D0831652

Political Religion and the Death of God

# Political Religion and the Death of God

Linda C. Raeder

✚

Sanctuary Cove Publishing
Palm Beach and Richmond

Copyright © 2017 by
Linda C. Raeder
Sanctuary Cove Publishing, N. Palm Beach FL 33410
Printed and bound in the United States of America
All rights reserved.

Library of Congress Cataloguing-in-Publication Data

Raeder, Linda C.
   Political Religion and the Death of God / Linda C. Raeder.
   Includes bibliographical references.
   ISBN 13-978-1545- 152218
Typeface:  Garamond Pro

In loving memory of my father,

Howard M. Maxwell

# Contents

# Acknowledgements

I am indebted above all to the many students at Palm Beach Atlantic University in West Palm Beach, FL who participated in my courses in political philosophy over the past sixteen years. This work would not appear in its present form without the knowledge and understanding I have gained through my experience teaching undergraduates at PBA. I would like to thank all those students who shared their perspectives and insights over the years and provided indispensable feedback to the ideas presented in this work.

I am further indebted to the PBA administration, particularly President Bill Fleming and Dr. Ken Mahanes, both of whom have provided unwavering support and encouragement for my scholarship and teaching. My colleagues in the Politics Department, Dr. Francisco Plaza and Dr. James Todd, have also earned my deepest gratitude, not only for their graciousness and collegiality, but also for the penetrating insight and maturity of vision that mark their scholarship and teaching.

Thank you as well to my mother, Evelyn Pokorny Maxwell, for her steadfast love, support, and strength, and my dear animal companions, Max, Sophie, Callie, and the Muscovies, who make day-to-day existence a continual joy.

Political Religion and the Death of God

*Let me say . . . that this conception of the state, that it is merely a police force, is, to my mind, a wholly erroneous conception; . . . the state is something far higher and more godlike than this . . . If we could only invest it in our thought with its true divine character, we should need no other agency for the unification of society.* —Washington Gladden

*'On earth there is nothing greater than I: it is I who am the regulating finger of God'.—thus roareth the monster.*

—Friedrich Nietzsche

The most significant political development in the United States over the past century has been the gradual but incessant growth of government and corresponding transformation of American constitutional order. Several related trends have contributed to such a development. The growth of government is partly due to the ever-wider embrace of socialist or quasi-socialist ideals among the American electorate, including the pursuit of social justice and correlative belief that government possesses the right and responsibility to override the market process through various forms of economic intervention. It is also a consequence of the greater demands placed upon government by the American people. The modern corruption of language bemoaned by Orwell and others has played a role as well, resulting in significant changes in the meaning of various concepts central to American moral and political discourse—law, rights, justice, equality, tolerance, and others—and corresponding degeneration of constitutionalism and the rule of law. Such factors, like the rise of moral consequentialism, subjectivism, and relativism, are not isolated phenomena but rather particular

1

manifestations of a more general and far-reaching change in Western and American culture, namely, change in religious belief and practice.

We have previously discussed the fact that every culture is ultimately informed by the implicit and explicit presuppositions, beliefs, and values—the worldview—held by its members, including and especially assumptions regarding the nature and purpose of existence embodied in religion, broadly conceived. The word cult, as we recall, originally referred to religious association or practice, pointedly indicating the inextricable link between religious belief and culture. We have also explored the formative influence of biblical religion on Western civilization. The unique civilization that emerged in the West—Christendom— received its characteristic identity through the profound impress of biblically based assumptions, values, belief, and practice. As we have seen, the United States Constitution, to take but one of innumerable instances, is incomprehensible without recognition of the Judeo-Christian worldview that tacitly informs its substance. The biblical presuppositions underlying the Constitution were taken for granted throughout much of American history. As the Illinois Supreme Court remarked in 1883, ". . . [o]ur laws and our institutions must necessarily be based upon and embody the teachings of the Redeemer of Mankind. It is impossible that it should be otherwise. And in this sense and to this extent, our civilization and our institutions are emphatically Christian. . . ."[1] As President Calvin Coolidge further observed, "[the] foundations of our society and our government rest so much on the teachings of the Bible that it would be difficult to support them if faith in these teachings would cease to be practically universal in our country."[2] Similar historical

---

[1] Illinois Supreme Court, *Richmond v. Moore,* 107 Ill. 429, 1883 WL 10319 (Ill.), 47 Am. Rep. 445.
[2] Cited in Lee Hallman, *A Patriot's Devotional* (Author House, 2015)

observations could be repeatedly almost endlessly. The characteristic values and institutions of Western civilization, and most emphatically its American expression, were definitively shaped by the Judeo-Christian vision of existence. They are both a product of, and implicitly dependent upon, the unique spiritual foundation comprised by the biblical worldview. *The Death of God*

The Judeo-Christian worldview that decisively informed the development of Western civilization, as we have seen, has encountered profound challenge over the past several centuries. The French Revolution of 1789 represented in part a militant revolt against the religious traditions of the West, a revolt carried forward with growing intensity in the nineteenth century. Indeed, by the end of that century the celebrated German philosopher Friedrich Nietzsche could famously announce: "God is dead . . . And we have killed him," thereby providing postmodern or post-Christian Western society with its defining symbol—the "death of god."[3] We have discussed the socialist assault on traditional liberal society that rose to prominence in the nineteenth century, an assault accompanied by simultaneous attack on biblical religion, most prominently, Christianity. Reformers as diverse as Rousseau, Mill, and Marx recognized that traditional Christian commitments posed insurmountable barriers to achievement of their goals. Fabian socialists in

---

[3] "God is dead. God remains dead. And we have killed him. How shall we comfort ourselves, the murderers of all murderers? What was holiest and mightiest of all that the world has yet owned has bled to death under our knives: who will wipe this blood off us? What water is there for us to clean ourselves? What festivals of atonement, what sacred games shall we have to invent? Is not the greatness of this deed too great for us? Must we ourselves not become gods simply to appear worthy of it?" Friedrich Nietzsche, *Thus Spoke Zarathustra: A Book for Everyone and No One*, R.J. Hollingdale, ed and trans (London: Penguin Classics, (1961 [1883]).

England and their Progressive counterparts in the United States were similarly concerned to weaken or redefine traditional Christian commitments and for similar reasons. The ascendancy of the socialist moral ideal over the course of the nineteenth century also influenced internal developments within certain Christian denominations in the direction of socialist ethics, mostly notably, the Social Gospel movement.[4]

The explicit and implicit attack on Christianity was accompanied, moreover, by construction of various novel "religions" or quasi-religions intended to serve as replacements for biblical faith. Nineteenth-century critics of classical-liberal society well understood the importance of religion to culture. Many such thinkers were particularly cognizant of the role played by religion in establishing bonds of social cohesion or unity. They recognized that the demise of Christianity, regarded by its critics as both justified and salutary, would nevertheless create a spiritual void for the millions upon millions of Christianized peoples comprised by Western society. They further recognized that such spiritual disorientation would threaten the existential sense of meaning and purpose requisite to social order. Accordingly, such thinkers concluded, mere evisceration or elimination of Christianity, however necessary and beneficial, was insufficient. The religious void produced by the eighteenth century's critical attacks on Christianity must be filled by the propagation of new and different religious or quasi-religious aspirations. Thinkers such as Comte in France and J. S. Mill in England, among others, occupied themselves with the construction of precisely such a religious replacement for Christianity—the Religion of Humanity, the proximate forebear of contemporary Secular Humanism. The socialism

---

[4] Charles D. Cashdollar, *The Transformation of Theology (1830-1890)* (Princeton: Princeton University Press, 1989). Hereinafter cited as *Transformation of Theology*.

of Marx and fellow travelers would serve an identical quasi-religious purpose.[5]

The nineteenth century, then, witnessed powerful challenges to traditional biblical faith, its reinterpretation in the direction of socialist ethics, and construction of various forms of "secular" or "political religion" intended to supplant Judeo-Christian aspirations, beliefs, and values in the minds of the masses.[6] Modern political religion comprises forms as varied as classic communism, socialism, and fascism, the Social Gospel, the Religion of Humanity or Secular Humanism, and others. The particular secular or political religions vary in form but are united in inspiration, substance, and purpose. The aim of all such constructions is the reorientation of religious devotion away from its traditional locus—the *transcendent* God of the Western tradition—and toward one or another *immanent*, intra-worldly, or mundane entity. In the case of Marx, the transcendent God is supplanted by the immanent communist society of the future. The realization of communism, like the Christian *eschaton*, is characterized as the "end of history"—the goal toward which history is ineluctably moving and toward which all spiritual and material efforts are to be directed. Comte, Mill, and fellow travelers conceive the replacement for the Judeo-Christian God as the intra-worldly abstraction proposed by Comte—the so-called "Great Being of Humanity."[7] In this case, religious aspirations are to be reoriented away from the transcendent God and toward this-worldly "service to Humanity," a service, said Mill, which henceforth will

---

[5] Richard H. Crossman, ed, *The God That Failed* (New York: Columbia University Press, 2001) (hereinafter cited as *God That Failed*).

[6] See Linda C. Raeder, *John Stuart Mill and the Religion of Humanity* (Columbia, MO: University of Missouri Press, 2002). Hereinafter cited as *Religion of Humanity*.

[7] John Stuart Mill, *Auguste Comte and Positivism* (Ann Arbor: University of Michigan Press, 1968 [1865]), 136-137. Hereinafter cited as ACP.

supplant biblical ethics as the very "law of our lives." The German-Nazi version aimed to reorient religious devotion away from the God of the Bible and toward the realization, in this world, of the millennial reign of the Third Reich. Nietzsche, who witnessed the emergence and propagation of various such quasi-religious constructions, clearly perceived their significance: such representations symbolize not only the "death of God" but also the implicit transfer of divine status from God to Man. He perceived, more particularly, that the "death of God," in effect and in practice, entailed the transfer of divine status from God to the "state."[8] The state, government, the wielders of political power, said Nietzsche, had become the "New Idol," the worldly replacement for God: "'On earth there is nothing greater than I: it is I who am the regulating finger of God'.—thus roareth the monster."[9]

The most significant aspect of such efforts to replace biblical with secular or political religion—"a religion without a God," in the words of Mill—has been their success.[10] Christianity was significantly weakened, relegated to the private sphere of mere subjective preference, or rejected outright. The de-Christianization of the West has advanced more thoroughly in Europe than America, but American society has not been immune to modern and postmodern developments. The spiritual vacuum created by the "death of God" was filled on both continents by the modern ideological movements and their descendants and fellow travelers. Communism, socialism, fascism, English Fabianism, Social Gospel, and

---

[8] Henri de Lubac, *The Drama of Atheist Humanism* (San Francisco: Ignatius Press, 1995). Hereinafter cited as *Drama*.
[9] Nietzsche exclaims: "The state? What is that? Well then! Now open your ears, for now I shall speak to you of the death of peoples. , [t]he state is the coldest of all cold monsters. Coldly it lies, too; and this lie creeps from its mouth: "I, the state, am the people. . . . On earth there is nothing greater than I: it is I who am the regulating finger of God."—thus roareth the monster." Nietzsche, "The New Idol" in *Thus Spoke Zarathustra* (1883).
[10] Mill, *ACP*, 133.

contemporary movements such as liberal Progressivism, radical environmentalism, Liberation Theology, and others served, and serve, for many adherents as quasi-religious substitutes for traditional faith, that is, as political religions. The moral ethos that typically accompanies the various modern forms of political religion similarly assumes various forms, including utilitarianism, naturalism, Marxian egalitarianism, Comtean altruism and positivism, secular humanism, postmodern perspectivism, and others. Such post-Christian moral constructions, like the modern political religions, vary in form but are united by a common and characteristic attribute, namely, rejection of a theological *source* of morality. All post-Christian moral constructs regard human beings, in one way or another, as the exclusive authors of right and wrong. As one disciple of secular humanism succinctly expressed the essence of post-theological, secular, or naturalistic ethics, "Man is his own rule and his own end."[11]

We have said that the most important aspect of the novel religious and moral constructions accompanying the "death of God" has been their social success. Marx's particular construction was so influential as to have become more or less synonymous with the twentieth century, the Age of Ideology. Unadulterated Marxism was undoubtedly too strong a brew for American tastes. Its underlying anti-theological ethos was nevertheless conveyed to the United States in somewhat less virulent forms, including secular humanism and other varieties of nontheistic, naturalistic, and "social" ethics, embraced chiefly but not exclusively by its political, intellectual, and cultural elite. It is rarely recognized or acknowledged, however, that secular humanism (the Religion of Humanity), along with similar non-theological ethical constructs, was expressly conceived by its founders and advocates as a rival to Christianity, which was explicitly and

---

[11] J. Wesley Robb, *The Reverent Skeptic: A Critical Inquiry into the Religion of Secular Humanism* (New York: Philosophical Library, 1979.

rightly regarded as the chief competitor of the new Humanitarian faith.[12] It is not coincidental that every religion but traditional biblical religion is tolerated in the contemporary American public square, including the public schools.

The modern and postmodern transformation of Western religious and moral beliefs—the replacement of biblical with secular or political religion and relocation of the source of morality from God to Man—has had, and continues to have, immense repercussions for Western and American society. Religion of course touches upon the most profound of existential questions and fulfills perhaps the most essential of human needs—the individual's need to find meaning and purpose in existence. Contrary to the assertions of nihilism, no human being can live without meaning and without purpose. Man by nature is not only a rational and social being, as the Western tradition long recognized, but also a religious being. No human being can avoid the fundamental existential questions: Who am I? Where did I come from? What am I doing here? Where am I going? Every society known to history, from ancient Sumer to modern America, has sought answers to such questions, answers embodied in its religion. The very term (from the Latin *religare*—to fasten or bind*)* points clearly to the human need for connection with the source of existence.[13] We have seen that it is impossible not to embrace a religion in this broad sense. Atheism too purports to answer the fundamental religious questions—where did I come from, where I am going? However unsatisfactory its response ("nowhere") may appear to persons of traditional religious views, its denial of God nevertheless aims to guide the human quest for existential comprehension.

That said, however, it is clear that not all religions are created equal. Religious truth of course involves the greatest

---

[12] Raeder, *Religion of Humanity.*

[13] There is some dispute regarding the etymology of the term but this is the sense favored by Christian thinkers such as Augustine.

and thorniest of all possible quests for knowledge. Ultimate Truth regarding man's relation to God must ever remain a perennial quest and not the absolute possession of any human being. Despite such irremediable ignorance on the part of every human being, the Western mind has nevertheless believed it possible to differentiate religion according to the degree to which it captures or fails to capture the higher truth of existence. A particular religion may be true or false, more true than false or more false than true, a judgment which depends on the degree to which it embodies the truth of reality. Of particular relevance in this regard is the distinction made by scholars such as Eric Voegelin (1901-1985) between transcendent and immanent (cosmological) religion. The early Greek philosophers are generally credited with the philosophical differentiation of existence into two dimensions: the "intelligible" realm—the transcendent realm of existence "Beyond" (*epekeina*) or above this world—and the "sensible" realm—the immanent realm of existence "within" the world. The great world-historical religions, Judaism, Christianity, and Islam, all conceive God as Being who simultaneously transcends and dwells within the immanent world, who, in the language of the Greeks, exists beyond and within the mundane realm of normal worldly experience.

The biblical worldview embodies such a differentiation in the most profound sense. We have previously discussed the political significance of the dual allegiance implicit in the Judeo-Christian worldview (God and Caesar) and the dual jurisdictional authority that ultimately developed within Christendom (church and state). More generally, however, the Christian revelation deepened the experience of transcendence and immanence first apprehended and articulated by Greek philosophers. Christianity more fully elaborated the transcendent nature of God and eternity, inevitably bringing into greater relief the relatively more limited significance of experience in time, "within" this world, and ultimately leading to the existential transformation of Christian consciousness. Christian man had to learn to maneuver simultaneously in

9

two dimensions of experience, this world (*mundus*) and the other world (the Beyond). Religious experience always involves existential contact with the higher reality of God, a reality experienced by Christian consciousness as transcendent, beyond this world. The experience of transcendent Being, however, can be problematic for human consciousness. The problem is that religious seekers who have gained experience of the transcendent reality of God must nevertheless and simultaneously continue to exist *within* the immanent or mundane world. Newly Christianized consciousness had to learn to balance existence-in-time with existence-out-of-time. To avoid potential disorientation and destabilization, Christian man had to learn to negotiate what Voegelin, following Plato, calls the "tension" of life in the *metaxy*—the "in-between.'[14]

Such metaphysical discursions may seem far removed from the topic under discussion—the rise of political religion in modern Western society. According to Voegelin, however, they are profoundly implicated in that development. We have seen that biblical religion was widely and successfully challenged in the eighteenth and nineteenth centuries, a challenge, indeed, that continues to the present day. The result was the weakening or reinterpretation of traditional faith in the transcendent God of the Bible. The religious yearning of Western man, however, did not die alongside the "death of God." Many persons responded to the existential despair inevitably created by the loss of God by turning toward the substitute meaning and purpose promised by one form or another of political religion. Early adherents to the new socialist faith, for instance, amply testify to the quasi-

---

[14] Eric Voegelin, "Reason: The Classic Experience," in *Published Essays, 1966-1985 1990*), vol. 12 of *The Collected Works of Eric Voegelin*, ed. Ellis Sandoz (Baton Rouge: Louisiana State University Press, 1990), 289-90; *Order and History, Volume IV: The Ecumenic Age*, vol. 17 of *The Collected Works of Eric Voegelin*, ed. Michael Franz (Columbia, MO: University of Missouri Press, 2000), 408.

religious fulfillment they experienced from their newfound pursuit of "heaven-on-earth"—the earthly paradise promised by socialism and communism.[15] Western religious devotion has traditionally been oriented toward a God *beyond* this world in the hope and expectation of ultimate fulfillment *beyond* time, in eternity. Political religion captures that devotion and expectation and reorients it away from the transcendent Beyond and toward this world, toward mundane or intra-worldly phenomena, in the case of socialism and communism, toward achieving the future Kingdom of God on earth.

Many advantages were promised to potential converts. For one thing, human beings would no longer have to cling to mere faith, to mere hope for ultimate fulfillment in eternity. Their yearning for justice, for instance, would no longer have to await divine judgment but could rather be fulfilled in this world. Socialism promised the achievement of justice, not in a perhaps fanciful "beyond" in eternity but rather here and now. Indeed it promised total justice—social justice—on earth and in time and by strictly human means. Nor would believers have to await death to experience spiritual transfiguration, as promised by Christianity. The political religions promised spiritual rebirth, transformation, transfiguration, here and now, on earth and in time. Human nature itself would be transformed under the socialist dispensation. In line with the Marxian theory of consciousness, as we recall, the establishment of socialist relations of production promised the eventual emergence of a new type of human being—Socialist Man, unselfish, cooperative, devoted to the common good. Goodness, equality, justice, the amelioration of all human suffering—heaven-on-earth—were said to be within human reach, in this world, in time, no longer relegated to a (possibly illusory) future state in eternity. All that is required to realize Heaven-on-Earth is the transformation of social, economic, and

---

[15] Crossman, *God that Failed.*

political reality by human will and action. The Kingdom of God is at hand: "Workers of the world unite!! You have nothing to lose but your chains!"[16]

The socialist evangel spoke directly to the religious needs and spiritual yearning of those persons whose faith in the traditional God of the West had been weakened or shattered by the modern assault on Christianity. Many of them replaced the loss of existential meaning and purpose that accompanied the "death of God" with the quasi-religious pursuit of the socialist heaven-on-earth. The Christian yearning for salvation was reinterpreted in political and temporal terms. Various "secular messiahs," from the St. Simonians to Hitler, Stalin, and others, arose to lead the masses to the Promised Land. The pursuit of political salvation undoubtedly provided existential comfort for the individuals it consumed. Their lives were no longer empty, without meaning or direction. Although religious devotion could no longer be oriented toward its traditional object, the transcendent God of the Bible, now "dead," it could be redirected toward an eminently worthy entity, toward a purpose larger than mere self, a political purpose. The Christian promise of individual or personal salvation was supplanted by the collective salvation promised by political religion. Salvation would lie not in unity with a moribund God but rather with Man, the "Great Being of Humanity," a unity to be achieved by collective realization of quasi-religious socialist ideals. More formally stated, modern political religion represents a corruption of the Christian *eschaton*. The "vertical" transcendence *beyond* the world promised by Christian faith is replaced by promise of a "horizontal" transcendence *within* this world, achieved by pursuit and realization of the final end of history, the Communist Paradise of the future. Transfiguration and salvation are relocated from eternity to time, from the

---

[16] Karl Marx, *The Communist Manifesto,* in Robert C. Tucker, *The Marx-Engels Reader,* 2nd ed (New York: W.W. Norton & Company, 1978).

transcendent Beyond to the immanent world. In Voegelin's celebrated phrase, all forms of modern political religion represent an "immanentization of the *eschaton*."

## The Balance of Consciousness

By measure of respect for human life, the twentieth century was an era of unprecedented horror. From the Russian Revolution through the two World Wars to the Chinese Cultural Revolution and Cambodian killing fields, millions upon millions of persons were oppressed, enslaved, or slaughtered by revolution, war, and explicit policy of their own governments. Such widespread disorder demands explanation. One of the more persuasive and profound explorations of the political convulsions that plagued the Age of Ideology and Totalitarianism was offered by Voegelin. He argues that the ideological movements bound up with the modern catastrophe were neither random and inexplicable outbursts nor solely products of particular material and historical conditions. Such phenomena are instead bound up with the nature of modernity itself, in particular, with the religious developments under discussion. Voegelin argues that the ideological constructions that accompanied the "death of God" should be understood as the extreme manifestation of a general form of spiritual or psychic disorientation prevailing in the modern Western world. The crisis of modernity, he says, is in essence a spiritual crisis rooted in a deformation of the truth of reality.[17]

Voegelin, as mentioned, characterizes human existence as always and everywhere "existence-in-tension," existence in the "in-between" reality which Plato termed the *metaxy* and which

---

[17] Portions of this section first appeared in Linda C. Raeder, "Voegelin on Gnosticism, Modernity, and the Balance of Consciousness," *Political Science Reviewer*, Vol. XXXVI, 2007. I would like to thank the publisher for permission to use the material in this book. Hereinafter cited as "Balance of Consciousness."

is constituted by a simultaneous tension toward mundane, worldly, existence and its transcendent divine ground beyond this world. Human consciousness finds itself embedded within a mysterious, participatory reality "halfway between God and man." The experience of human consciousness comprises a simultaneous pull toward the existential poles of transcendence and immanence (*beyond* and *within* the world), the poles of immorality and mortality, knowledge and ignorance, perfection and imperfection, timelessness and time, spirit and matter, existence and non-existence, life and death, truth and its deformation.[18] Reality is a comprehensive whole that consists of both transcendent and mundane dimensions, of mutual participation of the divine and the human.

A "healthy," "balanced," or "well-ordered" consciousness, Voegelin maintains, is one that accepts the "tensional structure of existence" and mediates successfully between its opposing poles.[19] "Diseased" or "unbalanced" or "disordered" consciousness, on the other hand, may be defined as a mode of experience wherein one or the other of the existential poles whose tension constitutes the "in-between" reality of human existence has collapsed. It is existence within a truncated or deformed reality characterized by the eclipse of one or the other of its two inseparable dimensions. Disordered consciousness, then, may take one of two main forms, depending upon which existential dimension—the immanent or the transcendent—recedes from experience. The first possibility is the case wherein intense consciousness of transcendent reality (religious experience) serves to eclipse mundane reality. Voegelin terms such a condition one of "metastatic faith"—the belief in the imminent arrival of divine presence on earth in such a manner that worldly existence is

---

[18] Plato, cited in Eric Voegelin, "Reason: The Classic Experience," in *Anamnesis*, trans. and ed. Gerhart Niemeyer (Columbia, MO: The University of Missouri Press, 1978), 103.

[19] Voegelin, "Reason," 100.

transfigured. The second possible response to the tension inherent in human existence, and the one more problematic in the modern era, is the eclipse of the transcendent pole of existence by the illegitimate expansion of immanent to total reality. This world, the mundane world of time and space, is represented as Reality *in toto*; the transcendent dimension is obscured or denied. According to Voegelin, such is the existential response that underlies the various ideological constructions and other peculiarly modern and postmodern political and social movements.

Voegelin conceives the phenomenon of imbalanced consciousness as intimately related to humanity's spiritual advance from what he calls the "compact" spiritual experience of the ancient cosmological empires to the "differentiated" experiences bound up with classical philosophy and Christianity. The inhabitants of the cosmological empires, such as ancient Egypt, Persia, and Syria, experienced the Divine Source as an intra-cosmic entity and, accordingly, dwelled within a divinized "world full of gods." Their world was experienced as a microcosm that reflected the divine order of the cosmos, an order mediated through the political ruler to the people and the realm. Cosmological man did not yet differentiate or separate the divine and the immanent. He had not yet discovered either the soul or the transcendent Ground of Being, experiences which could dissociate the cosmos and the Ground into radically immanent and radically transcendent realms. Tension between the "truth of society" and the "truth of the soul" was undoubtedly experienced even in the compact societies. [20] Such tension, however, could not become socially disruptive so long as the cosmological order was experienced as all-embracing and so long as the existential

---

[20] The conventional self-interpretation of a society as it regards its existential role as representative of a higher truth; and universal humanity's existence under God, the discovery that the human psyche immediately participates in the Divine Source of order, respectively.

reality of the soul and the transcendent divine source remained undifferentiated.

The problem of unbalanced consciousness—the problem, as Michael Franz explains, "of maintaining a balance between openness to transcendent experience and sober attentiveness to the necessities of mundane existence"—is thus bound up with the "theophanic events" wherein the transcendent God revealed himself to man, beginning with the revelation of the "I Am" to the Hebrews.[21] Indeed, the prophet Isaiah is for Voegelin the prototypical bearer of metastatic faith—the "faith that the very structure of pragmatic existence in society and history is soon to undergo a decisive transformation."[22] Isaiah counseled the King to lay down his arms and trust that God would defeat his enemies. Isaiah's experience of the transcendent God was so intense as to eclipse the reality of political existence in time. He became convinced that divine intervention would transform the very structure of mundane reality in such a way as to ensure the victory of the Chosen People over their worldly enemies. Isaiah's experience of participation in divine transcendent reality was so strong that, according to Voegelin, he "tried the impossible—to make the 'leap in being' a leap out of existence into a divinely transfigured world beyond the laws of mundane existence."[23] Voegelin further argues that such a "prophetic conception of a change in the constitution of being," bound up as it with the existential discovery of the "truth of transfigured reality," lies at the root of the ideological consciousness that he regards as one of the main sources of disorder in the modern era.[24]

---

[21] Michael Franz, *Eric Voegelin and the Politics of Spiritual Revolt: The Roots of Modern Ideology* (Baton Rouge: Louisiana State University Press, 1992), 30.

[22] Ibid. 32.

[23] Ibid. 34.

[24] Ibid. Thomas J. J. Altizer, "A New History and a New But Ancient God," in Ellis Sandoz, ed, *Eric Voegelin's Thought: A Critical Appraisal* (Durham: Duke University Press, 1982), 184.

The classical philosophers also struggled with the problem of existential balance deriving from the discovery of spiritual order. The discoveries they made—of the transcendent nature of the divine source (the Platonic *epekeina* or Beyond) and of the psyche, the "human spiritual soul" that is the "sensorium of transcendence" —were epochal events in mankind's advance from spiritual dimness to spiritual clarity. Plato discovered that openness of the psyche toward divine reality may permit certain transcendent experiences that shape the order of soul and society. He discovered the transcendent Ground of Being that is the source of personal, social, and historical order. Voegelin contends, however, that Plato, unlike Isaiah, managed to maintain a balance of consciousness in the face of the theophanic event. He did not permit his transcendent experiences to disturb his awareness of the autonomous structure of mundane reality, of the enduring reality of existence in the cosmos-of-begetting-and-perishing. Although Plato glimpsed a realm of enduring perfection, he remained lucidly aware of both the "improbability" of its establishment in time and the inevitable decline of such a perfect order if it were somehow to come into being. Platonic philosophy thus represents for Voegelin a model of "noetic control," of healthy, balanced existence within the enduring tensions of the *metaxy*.

Although the Platonic discovery was an advance from compactness to differentiation, it was, according to Voegelin, but a step on the spiritual path that found its end in the epiphany of Christ. Christianity, for Voegelin, represents the "maximal differentiation" of the relation between God and man. The "leap in being" that accompanied the epiphany of Christ fully differentiated the transcendent nature of the divine source and the truth of transfigured reality. The effect was not only to heighten the tension of existence in the *metaxy* but also potentially destabilize the balance of consciousness, as previously mentioned. It is perhaps difficult for modern man to re-experience the "shock" felt by those who first experienced the revelation of the transcendent God and the concomitant "withdrawal of Divinity from the world." The newly de-divinized cosmos, in contrast to the "world full of gods" experienced within cosmological society, must have "seemed to be left an empty shell, void of meaning, [indeed,] void of reality."[25] Christianity, Voegelin observes, further "reordered human existence in society . . . through the experience of man's destination, by the grace of the world-transcendent god, towards eternal life in beatific vision."[26] In light of such experiences, as we have seen, the value, meaning, and significance of mundane existence could only appear diminished or limited. In Voegelinian terms, the Christian revelation challenged the existential balance of consciousness. The modern ideological movements, which he regards as manifestations of existential imbalance and disorientation, are thus intimately bound up with the Christian experience. It is not accidental that such movements arose within Western civilization, within Christendom.

*Gnosticism and Modernity*

From the seventh century B.C. onward the ancient Near East was racked by a series of military conquests that profoundly disoriented the inhabitants of the various cosmological empires. A widespread sense of meaningless and psychic disorientation was engendered by the slaughter, enslavement, and forced intermingling of peoples and cultures, inevitably undermining faith in the traditional cosmological order. Various responses arose in the attempt to comprehend the meaning of existence within such a troubled world, among the more important of which were Stoicism, Christianity, and Gnosticism.

---

[25] William C. Havard, "Voegelin's Diagnosis of the Western Crisis," *Denver Quarterly* X (1975), 129-30.

[26] Eric Voegelin, *The New Science of Politics: An Introduction* (Chicago: The University of Chicago Press, 1952), 107.

To the Gnostics of the era, the world appeared neither as the "well-ordered" cosmos of the Greeks nor as the Judeo-Christian world that God created *ex nihilo* and "found good." On the Gnostic view, by contrast, the world appeared as a "prison from which [man must] escape, . . . an alien place into which man has strayed and from which he must find his way back home to the other world of his origins."[27] The fundamental experience of the ancient Gnostics was of an alien, disorganized, chaotic, and meaningless world. God was experienced as an absolutely transcendent entity utterly divorced from mundane existence, the existing world as false, devoid of reality, as "existent nothingness." Not surprisingly, the central theme of the diverse Gnostic thinkers was the "destruction of [such an abhorrent] old world and the passage to [a] new."[28] A new world, one that offers salvation from an old world felt to be wrong in its very constitution, could be gained, they taught, through personal effort and a privileged *gnosis* (knowledge) of the means of escape.

According to Voegelin, the ancient Gnostic speculations engendered in response to the disorder of the "ecumenic age" are significant because the experiences and beliefs they symbolize have re-emerged in modernity with such force as to decisively have shaped the character of that era. The history of modernity, he argues, is the history of a struggle between two different representations of the truth of existence: the representation of the truth of the soul and of man's relationship to God as manifested in classical philosophy and Christianity, on the one hand, and, on the other, the "new truth" propounded by modern gnostic thinkers—the alleged truth of the radical immanence of existence and the promise of revolutionary transfiguration of man and society in time.[29]

---

[27] Eric Voegelin, *Science, Politics, and Gnosticism*m (Chicago: Henry Regnery Company, 19678), 9.

[28] Ibid. 10.

[29] Voegelin uses the term "gnosticism" in an unconventional and very broad sense. It is his term for certain disorders of the spirit

Greek philosophy, as we have seen, discovered the truth of transcendent divinity, a truth decisively differentiated by the epiphany of Christ. The Christian revelation particularly effected an "uncompromising [and] radical de-divinization of the world" and a concomitant dissociation of previously unified spiritual and temporal power, as previously discussed.[30] Henceforth the transcendent spiritual destiny of man was to be existentially represented by the Church and the de-divinized temporal sphere of political power by the Empire, a "double representation of man in society" which endured through the Middle Ages and beyond.[31]

Voegelin maintains that the philosophic and Christian truth of man in society was challenged during the late Middle Ages by the rise of various gnostic spiritual movements. Such would prove to be the seedbed of the modern ideological consciousness that ultimately effected the "re-divinization" of political society in the name of a new truth of existence (cf. Nietzsche's "New Idol"). The medieval movements, according to Voegelin, were an outgrowth of a division within the early Christian community that stemmed from varying interpretations of the Revelation of St. John. The Revelation had aroused chiliastic expectations among certain early Christians, and they impatiently awaited Christ's imminent Second Coming. Augustine had sought to dash such expectations by re-interpreting John. Christ's thousand-year

---

arising from "pneumapathological" or imbalanced consciousness. It is more or less synonymous with other terms Voegelin employs to symbolize the phenomenon of spiritual disorder: "activist dreaming, egophantic revolt, metastatic faith, activist mysticism, demonic mendacity, Prometheanism, parousiasm, political religion, social Satanism, magic pneumatism, and eristics" (Franz, 17).

[30] Voegelin, *New Science*, 100.

[31] Gregor Sebba, "History, Modernity, and Gnosticism," in Peter J. Opitz and Gregor Sebba, eds, *The Philosophy of Order: Essays on History, Consciousness and Politics* (Stuttgart: Ernst Klett, 1981), 231.

reign on earth, he declared, had already begun with the Incarnation; thus "there would be no divinization of society beyond the pneumatic presence of Christ and his Church."[32] According to the Augustinian philosophy of history, the period following the epiphany of Christ was the last of six historical phases, the *saeculum senescens*—a time of waiting for the end of history to be brought about through eschatological events. Augustine, moreover, had drawn a further distinction between profane and sacred history; the latter, in turn, was embedded in a transcendental history of the *civitas dei*, the City of God. Only transcendental history, including the sacred history of the epiphany of Christ and the establishment of the Church, had direction toward eschatological fulfillment. Profane history had no such direction or, indeed, meaning of any sort; it was merely a waiting for the end in a radically "de-divinized" world.

*The End of History*

The twelfth century, as previously noted, was a time of civilizational expansion and growth. Population increased, trade and settlement expanded, urban culture and intellectual life flourished. In the midst of such expansive vitality, Augustine's conception of a "senile" age seemed incongruous, and, at this critical juncture, a new construction of history emerged to challenge the Augustinian interpretation. The Calabrian monk Joachim of Flora (1135-1202) created a speculative history that satisfied the desire to endow mundane existence with a meaning which Christianity, and especially the Augustinian conception of history, had denied it. He did so by relocating the end of transcendental history—the Christian *eschaton*, the ultimate transfiguration in God out of time—within historical existence. Joachim's project, according to Voegelin, was the "first Western attempt at an

---

[32] Ibid.

immanentization of the meaning of history."[33] What begins with Joachim is a conception of Western society "as a civilizational course that comes into view as a whole because it is moving intelligibly toward an end."[34] Thus begins the modern attempt to find a Final End of mundane history that would substitute for the end of history in the transcendent Christian sense.

Joachim modeled his novel conception of history on the Trinity, dividing the course of history into three ages—the Age of the Father, the Son, and the Holy Spirit. The Age of the Father was said to span the beginning of creation to the time of Christ; the Age of the Son began with Christ and ended in Joachim's time; the Age of the Holy Spirit was about to dawn (Joachim predicted it would begin in 1260) and would last indefinitely. According to Voegelin, Joachim's construction is significant because the three-age symbolism he created rules not only the modern ideological constructions of history but also the "self-interpretation of modern [Western] society" and thus the structure of its politics to the present day. Joachitic history, which allowed immanent history to end with the End of sacred history (transfiguration in God), says Voegelin, was "fallacious, but not un-Christian." In the several centuries following Joachim's construction, the novel historical expectations he raised remained more or less within the Christian orbit; the anticipated increase of fulfillment in history was to come about through a new eruption of transcendent spirit. Over time, however, the process of "fallacious immanentization" begun by Joachim became more and more radical and the relation to transcendence ever more tenuous. By the eighteenth century, the increase of meaning in history would be conceived as a radically intra-mundane phenomenon; the transcendent pole that sustains the balance of existential consciousness collapsed. The result, according to

[33] Voegelin, *New Science*, 119.
[34] Ibid. 128.

Voegelin, is the spiritual and temporal disorder and disorientation of the so-called "modern" age.[35]

Voegelin further argues that the various manifestations of such spiritual disorder (he cites Marxism, National Socialism, fascism, positivism, progressivism, psychoanalysis, and modern liberalism) are united by a common attribute, namely, a radical "will to immanentization." All such constructions involve a closure toward the transcendent dimension of human experience. We previously noted another such common attribute —the rejection of a theological source of morality; the demand for a "purely human" ethics, as Mill put it, clearly manifests the Voegelinian "will to immanentization."[36] Indeed, the most extreme modern ideologies go a step further. Their proponents not only aim to obscure the transcendent ground of existence but further seek to transform the nature of being itself. As Voegelin explains, the aim is to "abolish the constitution of being, with its origin in divine, transcendent being, and to replace it with a world-immanent order of being."[37] In other words, and as previously discussed, the radical ideological constructions anticipate the transfiguration of human nature through human action in history, in particular, the spiritual rebirth anticipated by establishment of a terrestrial paradise endowed with the meaning and salvific qualities of the Christian *eschaton*. The Christian conception of man's ultimate transfiguration in God is brought "down to earth," transformed into the promise of human transfiguration in time accomplished through strictly human and immanent action. The transcendent Christian end of history is transformed into a mundane "End

---

[35] Voegelin maintains that the symbol of a "modern age" was created precisely to denote the "epoch marked by the decisive victory of the gnostics over the forces of Western tradition in the struggle for existential representation" (New Science, 134).

[36] J. S. Mill, "On Liberty," ed, Elizabeth Rapaport (Indianapolis: Hackett Publishing Company, Inc., 1976), 48.

[37] Voegelin, *New Science*, 121.

of History" to be concretely realized in the immanent future, within the world. The ideologists carried the process begun by Joachim to its limit; the transcendent dimension of reality was fully absorbed into mundane existence. Karl Marx is of course characteristic.

*Gnostic Symbolism*

Voegelin contends, then, that the modern ideological constructions are productions of "speculative gnostics" who share certain basic beliefs, existential motivations, and aims with their ancient forebears. These include:

1. Dissatisfaction with present existence.
2. Belief that such dissatisfaction is caused by the intrinsically poor organization of the world. If something is not right, the reason is to be found in the evil of the world.
3. Belief that salvation from the wickedness of the world is possible.
4. Belief that the order of being will be changed in an historical solution, that a good world will evolve over time.
5. Belief that a change in the order of being can be realized through human action, that "self-salvation," salvation through man's own effort, is possible.
6. Construction of a formula for personal- and world-salvation based upon knowledge of how to alter being. The gnostic thinker typically presents himself as a prophet proclaiming knowledge regarding the salvation of mankind.

The ancient and modern gnostics, then, share certain characteristic traits, but they also differ in certain respects. Most important, the moderns typically assume an aggressive, activist stance toward the putative evil of existent reality; the ancients, by contrast, were relatively quietist. Despite their disparate stances, Voegelin maintains that the experiential motivations and aims of ancient and modern gnostics are nevertheless of a piece. All gnostics experience the world "as a place of total chaos which would be transformed into a world of perfected, durable order by divine or human intervention. . . ."[38] All gnostics aim to alter the constitution of being through human effort in order to escape a world experienced as alien and evil and to do so by applying their special gnosis to that task. All of them falsely extrapolate their experience of the "Beyond" to the "Beginning," claiming knowledge of the nature and meaning of human existence and of history-as-a-whole that they do not and cannot actually possess. Modern gnostic ideologues also differ from their ancient counterparts in that the modern "revolt against reality" is directed against a world shaped by the Christian differentiation of spiritual truth. Accordingly, their constructions must be understood in light of the Christian background that informed their development.

Indeed, Voegelin maintains, the various modern ideologies may be said to "derive" from Christianity in that they represent immanentized transformations of Christian experience and symbolism, a derivation evidenced by their structural congruence with traditional Christian doctrine. First, all the modern ideologists adopted and transformed the Christian idea of perfection. For the Christian, life on earth is shaped by the expectation and aim of realizing a "supernatural [fulfillment] through grace in death."[39] The Christian idea of supernatural perfection thus consists of two components: a *teleological* (*telos*, final end or purpose) movement toward a final *axiological* goal (the state of ultimate perfection or "highest value"). We have seen that the ideological constructs immanentize the Christian *eschaton* by aiming to produce a final state of perfection within historical existence (axiological), a perfect society to be created through

---

[38] William C. Harvard, "Notes on Voegelin's Contributions to Political Theory," in Ellis Sandoz, ed, *Eric Voegelin's Thought: A Critical Appraisal* (Durham, NC: Duke University Press, 1982), 97-98.

[39] Voegelin, *New Science*, 105.

implementation of the ideologue's particular program or system (teleological). The ideological constructions differ, however, according to their varying emphases on the teleological and axiological elements of the Christian conception from which they derive. Accordingly, Voegelin classifies the various immanentist constructions under several heads:

1. *Teleological immanentization.* When the teleological component of the idea of perfection is immanentized, the main emphasis of the system lies on the forward movement toward the goal of perfection in this world. According to Voegelin, the eighteenth century ideal of "progress" is of this type, as is liberal progressivism in general. The emphasis is on movement; typically there is little clarity about the final state to be realized ("Change, change, change!").

2. *Axiological immanentization.* Here the emphasis is placed on the state of perfection in the world. Generally the thinker paints a detailed picture of the proposed perfect society while giving short shrift to the means by which it is to be realized. All formulations of "ideal societies" fall into this category. Thomas More's *Utopia* is a classic example.

3. *Activist Mysticism.* In this form of immanentization, the teleological and axiological types are combined. Here the thinker typically provides a more or less clear picture of the final state to be achieved as well as 'knowledge" of the means by which it is to be brought into existence. Comte's final state of industrial society under rule of managers and positivists is one example; Marx's communist society to be ushered in by the proletarian revolution is another.

The second set of Christian symbols transformed by the modern ideological speculators derives from the Joachitic conception of history previously discussed. Joachim created and bequeathed to modern man a complex of four symbols.[40] The first is that of the "Third Realm"—the third "world-historical phase that is at the same time the last, the age of fulfillment." Such symbolism reappears at a later date in various forms: the now-familiar distinction among ancient, medieval, and modern historical periods; the Comtean periodization of history into the theological, metaphysical, and positivist states of man; Marx's division of history into primitive communism, bourgeois class society, and the final realm of the classless Communist society; the Third Reich symbolism adopted by the Nazis; and so forth. The second symbol derived from Joachitic trinitarian eschatology was the symbol of the leader, the *dux*, who "appears at the beginning of each new era and establishes it through his appearance." This symbol also reemerges in various guises throughout the ensuing centuries: the belief that St. Francis of Assisi would usher in the new Age of the Holy Spirit; the self-styled paracletes imbued with the spirit of God who led the various sectarian movements of the Renaissance and Reformation; Machiavelli's Prince; the charismatic leaders of the national-socialist and fascist movements. The third symbol created by Joachim and adopted by the ideological thinkers was that of the prophet, the precursor of each of the three ages. This symbol was transformed over time from the still-Christian conception of Joachim's era into the secular intellectual who knows the program for salvation from the evils of the world, who can predict the future course of world history and knows the meaning of that history (e.g., Comte, Hegel, Mill, Marx). The final symbol bequeathed by Joachim to the modern world was the "community of spiritually autonomous persons." Joachim believed that the Age of the Holy Spirit would witness highly spiritualized individuals existing in community without the mediation and support of institutions and organizations; he had in mind the monks. Such a notion

---

[40] Ibid. 111-13.

reappears in later times, for instance, as the Marxian and anarchist notion of the "withering away" of the state and the radical-democratic conception of a society of "autonomous" men.

## Gnostic Experience

"The substance of history," Voegelin maintains, "is to be found on the level of experiences, not on the level of ideas."[41] Accordingly, the logic of modern political developments, especially the rise of the ideological mass movements, is only apparent in light of the existential consciousness that engendered them. Such phenomena must be traced to their source in the experiences and motivations of their founders and followers, above all, the aforementioned "will to immanentization." The existential drive for immanentization, according to Voegelin, arises from a desire to assuage the tension of existence in the *metaxy* and to do so by eliminating one source of such tension—man's experience of the transcendent. We recall that for Voegelin human existence is existence-in-tension within the participatory reality constituted by the simultaneous pull toward both mundane existence and its transcendent divine ground. By definition, a healthy or well-ordered consciousness is one that successfully mediates between the existential poles of immanence and transcendence; a disordered consciousness does not so succeed. Modern ideological consciousness obscures or denies the transcendent dimension of reality (closure toward the divine ground) and may thus be regarded as a form of imbalanced or disordered consciousness in the Voegelinian sense.

Although there is no one "cause" of such a disturbed relation to reality, of "pneumopathological" or spiritually disordered consciousness, Voegelin's analysis highlights certain existential characteristics common to the various ideological

---

[41] Ibid. 125.

constructions. In all cases of ideological consciousness, he suggests, the lust for power has grown immense. In his words, the will to power of the thinker "has triumphed over the humility of subordination to the constitution of being." The principal aim of the ideological thinker, he says, is to "destroy the order of being, which is experienced as defective and unjust and through man's creative power to replace it with a perfect and just order." In order to destroy such a "defective" order, it must be conceived as susceptible of human intervention. Such a requirement rules out the created order of the Judeo-Christian God, which of course is impervious to human manipulation. The order of being must be conceived as under man's control, in other words, its "givenness . . . must be obliterated."[42] The acquisition of human control thus requires the "retroactive" destruction of the God whose existence would prevent man from fashioning the order of being to his liking. Consequently, the first and most important task of the ideological thinker, as Nietzsche succinctly put it, is to "murder God." The radical "will to immanentization" and the passion to abolish transcendent reality emerge from an unbounded desire for power over being, the pneumopathological wish and need to *be* God. According to the "logic" of the disordered soul, such a wish can be realized by destroying God; in some quasi-magical fashion, he "who murders god will himself become god." Thus, says Voegelin, the "murder of God is of the very essence of the gnostic recreation of the order of being."[43] He further acknowledges, however, that full comprehension of the modern ideological passion to murder God is, in the final analysis, inaccessible to the human mind. As Voegelin put it, "[b]eyond the psychology of the will to power we are confronted with the inscrutable fact that grace is granted or denied."[44] The search for an ultimate explanation of the

---

[42] Voegelin, *Science, Politics, and Gnosticism*, 107, 53.

[43] Ibid. 55.

[44] Ibid. 31.

emergence of the modern would-be gods founders on the ultimate mystery of man's relation to God.

*Existential Resistance, Ideology, and the Drive for Certainty*

Voegelin further emphasizes that the modern ideological thinkers do not necessarily *deny* the truth of reality but rather *resist* such truth. They may in fact be spiritually sensitive persons with an acute sense of transcendence.[45] The defiant modern gnostics who created the ideological systems, like the philosophers and prophets who created the symbolism of philosophy and Christianity, experience a reality that has eschatological direction, one that is moving beyond its present structure. Moreover, they know reality moves not only into an historical future but also toward a transcendent Beyond. Ideological concepts such as "transcendence into the future" clearly point to the distinction they intend to obscure (an existence that "comes to an end in time without coming to [a] final End out-of-time"[46]). The question is why the ideological resisters defy a truth which with they do not actually disagree. A related question concerns the experiential sources that have made resistance to the truth of reality a recurring force in history.

The existential resisters, says Voegelin, are dissatisfied with the lack of order they experience in personal and social existence. Such dissatisfaction is readily understandable. Human existence is afflicted with many miseries—hunger, arduous work, disease, early death, injustice—and painfully disoriented by rapid change (such as engendered by the modern scientific and industrial revolutions and the rise of

---

[45] J. S. Mill is a case in point. He vigorously denied the charge of atheism, insisting in no uncertain terms that the Religion of Humanity he championed but not only a real religion but better than any previous religion.

[46] Eric Voegelin, Volume Five, *In Search of Order* (Baton Rouge: Louisiana State University Press, 1987), 34.

capitalism). Ideological resisters, like many other persons, suffer from present disorder. More important, however, they further suffer from the discrepancy between that disorder and the higher, truer order which they also apprehend yet which seems beyond the possibility of realization. They are "disappointed with the slowness of the [transfiguring] movement in reality toward the order they experience as the true order demanded by the Beyond" and, moreover, morally outraged at the human misery entailed by such "slowness." Such experiences can lead to the conviction that something is "fundamentally wrong with reality itself." At such a point, the resister to disorder becomes a revolutionary who seeks to overturn the structure of reality itself. The "Beyond is no longer experienced as an effective ordering force," and the ideologist constructs a system that will replace the defective force.[47] The tension of existence in the *metaxy* dissolves.

According to Voegelin, there further exists an even deeper stratum of ideological resistance, one originating in the very structure of consciousness and especially its imaginative capacity. Imagination, for Voegelin, is the capacity that permits human beings to symbolize, articulate, and otherwise express their participatory experience within the "*metaxy* of divine-human movements and counter-movements." It is the capacity that makes a human being a "creative partner in the movement of reality toward its truth."[48] Such a creative imaginative force, however, can go awry if the creative *partner* forgets he is a *partner* and begins to regard himself as "the sole creator of truth." Underlying the ideologist's illusory belief that he can create a new reality merely through creating a new symbol or image is precisely such an "imaginative expansion of participatory into sole power."[49] The imaginative capacity of human beings means that they can confuse their personal images of reality with reality itself.

---

[47] Ibid. 36-37.
[48] Ibid. 26, 37.
[49] Ibid. 38.

The ideological thinker, as we have seen, aims to abolish existential reality and the constitution of being in order to deliver man from various perceived evils. The control of being, however, does not actually lie within his grasp; reality is not actually susceptible of human manipulation. Accordingly, as Voegelin puts it, "nonrecognition of reality is the first principle" of the ideological constructions.[50] In order to make his pathological constructions seem plausible, the thinker must imaginatively construct what Voegelin, following Robert Musil, calls a "second Reality," a transfigured "dream world" that replaces the First Reality he finds so unsatisfactory. The Second Reality will resemble the First Reality in many respects (otherwise it would be too patently absurd), yet the ideological constructor necessarily eliminates from his model certain inconvenient features of reality.[51] The ideologists vary in regard to which elements of reality are omitted. Such may include the primary experience of the cosmos (the begetting and perishing of all existent forms), as in all constructions that anticipate the "End of History"; the need for institutional constraints and incentives as in Marx; the human penchant for possession, as in More's *Utopia*, and so on. The point is that every ideological thinker constructs an imaginary dream-world that eliminates essential elements of reality as we know it.

The construction of ideological systems or programs does not, of course, permit actual control over being or reality but nevertheless provides a measure of gratification to those who pursue it. The ideological constructors, Voegelin maintains, gain the "fantasy satisfaction" of certain psychic needs, in particular, the need for "a stronger certainty about the meaning of human existence."[52] Ideologues and their

---

[50] Voegelin, *New Science*, 169.

[51] For instance, Marx's communist paradise; Comte's positivist industrial society; the thousand-year rule of the Aryan masters, the eternally peaceful order of liberal constitutionalism, and so forth.

[52] Voegelin, *New Science*, 107.

followers are comforted by the increased sense of certainty that accompanies their newfound knowledge; the pretense of knowing the future course of events provides a seemingly firmer, if illusory, basis for action. Voegelin maintains, then, that ideological thinkers are ultimately impelled to action by the inherent *uncertainty* of human existence, an existence wherein assurance of meaning and purpose is only to be gained by faith-engendered experiences. The painful uncertainty of human existence is assuaged by the construction of Second Realities and philosophies of history that envision an everlasting realm of bliss in time.

## *Christianity and the Ideological Movements*

We have seen that, according to Voegelin, the modern ideological movements are bound up with the heightened spiritual tension engendered by the Christian differentiation of reality. In particular, Christianity's further differentiation of the truth of the soul and clarification of man's relation to a transcendent God exacerbated the existential uncertainty that the ideological constructions serve to assuage. The Christian faith, on Voegelin's view, requires tremendous spiritual strength, providing, as it does, no assurance of the meaning or value of personal existence other than that attained by faith itself. It does not provide massively *certain* knowledge of the nature of being, of God, or the meaning of mundane events but only the hard truth that the "order of reality is essentially mysterious."[53] A faith whose very "essence is uncertainty," Voegelin suggests, may generate a chronic and intolerable anxiety among those who long for greater reassurance.[54] The fact that the Christian differentiation of the truth of the soul is "more accurate" may provide scant consolation to those who crave a more certain guarantee of meaning and purpose.

---

[53] Ibid. 68.
[54] Ibid. 122-23.

Voegelin further maintains that Christianity's widespread social success in the West brought many people into the Christian orbit who did not possess the spiritual stamina to endure the strain of existence demanded by a faith characterized by essential uncertainty. The result, he says, was that "great masses of Christianized men who were not strong enough for the heroic adventure of faith became susceptible to ideas that could give them a greater degree of certainty about the meaning of their existence than Christian faith." The reality of being as known by Christianity, he says, is difficult to bear; and many persons took flight into alternative spiritual constructs that permitted a seemingly "firmer grip on God" than afforded by Christian faith.[55] The modern flight into such alternate constructs, moreover, was not an entirely novel development; similar responses have appeared throughout history wherever the truth of the transcendent God had been differentiated. As Voegelin explains, the "temptation to fall from spiritual height that brings uncertainty into final clarity down to a more solid certainty of world-immanent, sensible, fulfillment seems to be a general human problem."[56] The Israelitic differentiation of the transcendent God is a case in point. Individuals who could not endure the demands placed upon the Chosen People fell back upon the still culturally viable polytheism of the surrounding society. In the late Middle Ages, the socially available spiritual alternative to a difficult Christianity was the "living culture" of the various underground gnostic movements, which, according to Voegelin, provided "experiential alternatives sufficiently close to the experience of faith but far enough from it to remedy the uncertainty of strict faith."[57]

More particularly, the "experiential alternatives" offered by the gnostic spiritual movements, the forebears of modern ideology, consisted of various attempts to "expand the soul to

---

[55] Ibid. 124.
[56] Voegelin, *Science, Politics, and Gnosticism*, 114.
[57] Voegelin, *New Science*, 124.

the point where god is drawn into the existence of man."[58] In other words, the aim of such efforts was self-divinization. As Voegelin explains, the aim was to "divinize [the person who undergoes the experience] by substituting more massive modes of participation in divinity for faith in the Christian sense."[59] Voegelin identifies three such kinds of experiences, intellectual, emotional, and volitional. The intellectual variant typically takes the form of a "speculative penetration" of the mystery of creation and existence; the Hegelian system is representative. The emotional variant assumes the form of an "indwelling of divine substance in the human soul," as in the experiences of the paracletic sectarian leaders. The third type, the volitional, manifests itself as an "activist redemption of man and society," classically illustrated by Comte and Marx. According to Voegelin, such existential self-divinization constitutes the "active core" of the immanentist eschatology that impelled the modern re-divinization of state and society, a process unfolding "from medieval immanentism through humanism, enlightenment, progressivism, liberalism, positivism, and Marxism."[60]

The example of Marx well illustrates the existential dynamics involved in the process of self-divinization. Marx, following Feuerbach, insisted that God was a "projection" of man's highest and best qualities into some illusory Beyond; man's task is to draw his projection of God back into himself. In so doing, man becomes conscious that he himself *is* god; man is transfigured into a kind of Nietzschean *Übermensch* ("superman"). According to Voegelin, Marxian transfiguration represents the extreme form of a "less radical medieval experience, which drew the spirit of God into man, while leaving God himself in his transcendence." The modern supermen of Comte, Marx, and Nietzsche did not emerge from a cloud but rather represent the end of the road to radical

---

[58] Ibid. 124.
[59] Ibid.
[60] Ibid.

"secularization" marked over previous centuries by such figures as the "godded man" of the English Reformation mystics and similar constructs.[61] "Modern secularism," Voegelin concludes, "should be understood as the radicalization of . . . earlier forms of [medieval and] paracletic immanentism, because the experiential divinization of man is more radical in the secularist case."[62] He perceives historical continuity between medieval and modern gnostic movements and continuity of experiential dynamic within all forms of gnostic consciousness.

We have seen that the overarching goal of the modern ideologues is to abolish the tensions of historical existence by obscuring or denying the transcendent dimension of existence. To that end, the truth of the open soul in tension toward the divine, as well as its symbolic representations--philosophy and Christianity--must be abolished. Such a strategy accounts for the marked hostility to both classical philosophy and Christianity that characterizes the peculiarly modern and postmodern strains of Western civilization. On Voegelin's view, however, Christianity is not altogether blameless in this regard. Over time, he maintains, it came to embrace an excessive doctrinization and dogmatism that served to eclipse the experiential foundation of Christian truth. The ossification of that truth in formalistic and literalistic theological and metaphysical doctrine led Christian symbols to become opaque; the existential truth they were intended to express became increasingly obscure. According to Voegelin, the erosion of the existential meaning behind Christian symbols is implicated in the rise of the modern ideological movements insofar as it "permitted gnostic

---

[61] Ibid. 126.
[62] Ibid.

symbols of reality to take over the representational function among the nation states of the Western world."[63]

Indeed the rise of gnostic consciousness has led to a gradual transformation of the meaning of the principal symbols by which Western civilization had ordered itself for a millennium. The Christian person, whose spiritual qualities we have discussed at length, became a mere "man," a world-immanent being who governs the universe through intellect and will, through science and pragmatic action. The highest-order goods of the Western tradition—the life of contemplative reason expressed in philosophy and the life of the spirit symbolized by the Church—were attacked as "false and anachronistic." Under the influence of the scientistic and positivistic "science" that stems from gnostic consciousness, the "real" contracted to that which is immanent and objectively measurable; man's spiritual needs were no longer regarded as grounded in the truth of reality or being. On Voegelin's view, the resulting experiential impoverishment partially accounts for the mass appeal of the modern political religions and corresponding re-sacralization of the state: "Men can allow the world to so expand that the world and the God behind it disappear. But they cannot thereby solve the problem of their existence, for it endures in every soul. Thus when the God behind the world is unseen, the contents of the world emerge as new gods."[64] We have previously discussed the modern emergence of the New Idol.

For Voegelin, however, the most devastating consequence of the modern gnostic victory is the "radical expurgation of a whole range of experiences previously open to man"—the symbolic experiences of transcendence through which the human being gains his sense of order, meaning, and immortality. Indeed, the loss of such experiences was both

---

[63] Eric Voegelin, *Political Religions,* trans. T. J. DiNapoli and E. S. Easterly III (Lewiston, NY: The Edwin Mellen Press, 1986), 50-51.

[64] Ibid.

cause and effect of the rise of revolutionary gnostic consciousness. The ossification of existential truth into dogma served to eclipse the living truth such dogma was meant to protect, creating an existential void to be filled by the gnostic promise. The radical immanentization that ensued served in turn to further suppress those intimations of order and meaning rooted in participation in the divine ground. Those who embraced the gnostic vision experienced a world deprived of any relation to transcendent being. The ensuing sense of confinement fanned the flames of revolt against the limits of such a closed existence and fueled the revolutionary drive to realize the impossible goal of intramundane perfection embodied in the modern political religions. The nightmare of the past century was created by disoriented souls railing against the prison-like confines of a closed or truncated reality.

The "unprecedented destructiveness" of the twentieth century was accompanied, paradoxically, by significant social achievement: growth in population accompanied by advances in material well-being, longevity, and literacy, much of which made possible by the development of science and technology. The contemporary age, Voegelin says, represents the curious phenomenon of a civilization that is "declining" and "advancing" at the same time. His analysis of modernity suggests that the simultaneous material growth and spiritual decline of Western civilization is related to the process of radical immanentization or "secularization" under discussion. As he explains, "gnostic speculation overcame the uncertainty of faith by receding from transcendence and endowing man and his intramundane range of action with the meaning of eschatological fulfillment; . . . as this immanentization progressed experientially, civilizational activity became a mystical work of self-salvation."[65] The modern "recession from transcendence" permitted the release of tremendous spiritual energy for the pursuit of worldly achievement; in building civilization, man felt himself to be earning salvation

---

[65] Ibid. 129.

itself. Insofar, however, as civilizational pursuits became a diversion from or substitute for genuine spirituality, the life of the spirit was vitiated. Insofar as intramundane activity "absorbed into itself the eternal destiny of man," the transcendent experiences that constitute the ultimate source of both personal and social order tended to disappear or become unintelligible. "The price of progress," Voegelin pessimistically concludes, "is the death of the spirit."[66]

Despite such a gloomy conclusion, however, Voegelin also leaves grounds for hope: Truth, in the end, must prevail. As he says, "[t]he closure of the soul in modern gnosticism can repress the truth of the soul . . . but it cannot remove the soul and its transcendence from the structure of reality." The flight from reality cannot last forever. Moreover, the eschatological interpretation of history results in a false picture of reality (the order of concrete human societies is not in fact an *eschaton*); and errors with regard to the structure of reality have practical consequences. One would think that the totalitarian nightmare of the twentieth century and eventual collapse of the former Soviet Union would give pause to even the most zealous ideologues. Tragically, however, that does not seem to be the case. Marxism, socialism, and efforts to remove Christianity from the public sphere, indeed, even from the private sphere, are alive and well in contemporary Western society, including American society. Moreover, the ideological constructs identified by Voegelin are not the only manifestations of the radical immanentization or secularization he decried. Other socially influential intellectual and spiritual paradigms and perspectives, including Progressivism, Social Gospel, Postmodernism, and Multiculturalism, have contributed, and continue to contribute, to erosion of the spiritual foundation of Western and American order.

---

[66] Ibid. 131.

## Bibliography

Acton, H.B. 2003. *The Illusion of the Epoch: Marxism-Leninism as a Philosophical Creed.* Indianapolis: Liberty Fund.

Billington, James. 1980. *Fire in the Minds of Men: Origins of the Revolutionary Faith.* New York: Basic Books.

Carey, George W. 1995. *In Defense of the Constitution.* revised and expanded. Indianapolis: Liberty Fund.

Cashdollar, Charles D. 1989. *The Trans formation of Theology, 1830-1890.* Princeton: Princeton University Press.

Cohn, Norman. 1970. *The Pursuit of the Millenium.* New York: Oxford University Press.

Corwin, Edward S. 2008. *The Higher Law Background of American Constitutional Law.* Indianapolis: Liberty Fund.

Crimmins, James E., ed. 1990. *Religion, Secularization, and Political Thought: Thomas Hobbes to J.S. Mill.* London: Routledge.

Crossman, Richard H., ed. 2001. *The God That Failed.* New York: Columbia University Press.

Dostoyevsky, Fyodor. 1993. *The Grand Inquisitor: with Related Chapters from the Brothers Karamazov.* Indianapolis: Hackett Publishing Comany, Inc.

Ekirch, Arthur. 2009. *The Decline of American Liberalism.* Oakland, CA: Independent Institute.

Ellul, Jacques. 1979. "Politization and Political Solutions." In *The Politicization of Society,* edited by Kenneth S. Templeton. Indianapolis: Liberty Press.

Evans, M. Stanton. 1994. *The Theme is Freedom: Religion, Politics, and the American Tradition.* Washington, D.C.: Regnery Publishing, Inc.

Franz, Michael. 1992. *Eric Voegelin and the Politics of Spiritual Revolt: The Roots of Modern Ideology* . Baton Rouge: Louisiana State University Press.

40

Frohnen, Bruce, ed. 2002. *The American Republic: Primary Sources.* Indianapolis: Liberty Fund.

Gamble, Richard. 2004. *The War for Righteousness: Progressive Christianity, the Great War, and the Rise of the Messianic Nation.* Wilmington, DE: Intercollegiate Studies Institute.

Hall, Daniel L. Dreisbach and Mark David, ed. 2009. *The Sacred Rights of Conscience.* Indianapolis: Liberty Fund.

Hamburger, Joseph. 1999. *John Stuart Mill on Liberty and Control.* Princeton: Princeton University Press.

Harp, Gillis. 2005. *Positivist Republic: Auguste Comte and the Reconstruction of American Liberalism, 1865-1920* . University Park, PA: Penn State University Press.

Hayek, F.A. 1991. *The Fatal Conceit: the Errors of Socialism.* ed W.W. Bartley III. Chicago, University of Chicago Press.

Hegel, G. W. F. 1929. *Hegel: Selections.* Edited by Jacob Loewenberg. New York: Scribner's Sons.

Hoffer, Eric. 1951. *The True Believer: Thoughts on the Nature of Mass Movements.* San Bernardino: Borgo Press.

Koenker, Ernest B. 1965. *Secular Salvations: The Rites and Symbols of Political Religions.* Philadelphia: Fortress Press.

Locke, John. 2003. *Two Treatises of Government and a Letter Concerning Toleration.* New Haven: Yale University Press.

Lubac, Henri de. 1995. *The Drama of Atheist Humanism.* San Francisco: Ignatius Press.

Löwith, Karl. 1949. *Meaning in History.* Chicago: University of Chicago Press.

Manuel, Frank E. 1983. *The Changing of the Gods.* Hanover, NH: Brown University Press.

—. 1956. *The New World of Henri Saint-Simon.* Cambridge: Harvard University Press.

41

Mazlish, Bruce. 1976. *The Revolutionary Ascetic: Evolution of a Political Type.* New York: McGraw-Hill.

Opitz, Edmund A. 1996. *Religion: Foundation of the Free Society.* Irvington-on-Hudson, NY: Foundation for Economic Education, Inc.

Orwell, George. 2010. *Politics and the English Language and Other Essays.* Oxford: Benediction Classics.

Pera, Marcello. 2011. *Why We Should Call Ourselves Christian.* New York: Encounter Books.

Pestritto, Ronald J. and William J. Atto, ed. 2008. *American Progressisvism: a Reader.* Lanham, MD: Lexington Books.

Pestritto, Ronald J. 2005. *Woodrow Wilson and the Roots of Modern Liberalism.* Lanham, MD: Rowman & Littlefield Publishers, Inc. Raeder, Linda C. 2002. *John Stuart Mill and the Religion of Humanity.* Columbia, MO: University of Missouri Press.Ryn, Claes G. 1992. "Political Philosophy and the Unwritten Constitution." *Modern Age* 303-309.

Raeder, Linda C. 2002. *John Stuart Mill and the Religion of Humanity.* Columbia: MO: University of Missouri Press.

Sebba, Gregor. 1981. "History, Modernity, and Gnosticism." In *The Philosophy of Order: Essays on History, Consciousness and Politics,* edited by Peter J. Opitz and Gregor Sebba. Stuttgart: Ernst Klett.

Shah, Timothy Samuel and Hertzke, Allen D., ed. 2016. *Christianity and Freedom. Vol. I: Historical Perspectives.* II vols. Cambridge: Cambridge University Press.

Shaw, G. Bernard. 1889. *Fabian Essays in Socialism.* London: Fabian Society.

Smith, Ronald Gregor. 1966. *Secular Christianity.* New York: Harper and Row.

Sowell, Thomas. 1987. *A Conflict of Visions: Ideological Origins of Political Struggles.* New York: William Morrow & Co.

Talmon, Jacob L. 1960. *Political Messianism.* New York: Frederick A. Praeger.

—. 1952. *The Rise of Totalitarian Democracy.* Boston: Beacon Press.

Thornton, Bruce S. 2007. *Decline and Fall: Europe's Slow Motion Suicide.* San Francisco: Encounter Books.

Turner, James. 1985. *Without God, Without Creed: the Origins of Unbelief in America.* Baltimore: Johns Hopkins University Press.

Viner, Jacob. 2015. *The Role of Providence in the Social Order: An Essay in Intellectual History.* Princeton: Princeton University Press.

Voegelin, Eric. 1986. *Political Religions.* Translated by T. J. DiNapoli and E.S. Easterly III. Edwin Mellen *Press.*

—. *1968. Science, Politics, and Gnosticism .* Chicago: Henry Regnery Company.

Witte, John Jr. 2005. *Religion and the American Constitutional Experiment.* 2nd. Boulder: Westview Press. right, T.R. 1986. *The Religion of Humanity: The Impact of Comtean Positivism on Victorian Britain.* Cambridge: Cambridge University Press.